Lost In Michigan's
Abandoned Places

◆ETAOIN PUBLISHING◆
www.etaoinpublishing.com

HURON
PHOTO.COM

Publisher:   Etaoin Publishing and Huron Photo LLC
             Saginaw, MI
             www.EtaoinPublishing.com
             www.HuronPhoto.com




Ordering Information:
Books may be ordered from www.LostinMichigan.net

Printed in the United States of America

ISBN 978-1-955474-25-2

# Introduction

Michigan, a state rich in history, has witnessed periods of rapid growth and decline. From the bustling days of the fur trade and lumber industry to the rise and fall of manufacturing, the state's economy has experienced significant shifts. These fluctuations have left behind a fascinating array of abandoned sites, each with its own unique story.

While these forgotten places may seem desolate, they continue to hold historical significance. They are not truly abandoned but remain under ownership, whether private, nonprofit, or governmental. This book focuses on sites accessible or visible to the public, offering glimpses into Michigan's past.

If you choose to explore these abandoned locations, it's crucial to approach them with respect. Adhere to posted signs and avoid entering closed-off or unsafe structures. By respecting these guidelines, you contribute to the preservation of these historical sites for future generations.

# Contents

# Chapter One
# Southern Lower Peninsula

# Chapter 2
## Central Lower Peninsula

# Chapter 3
## Northern Lower Peninsula

# Chapter 4
## Upper Peninsula

# Chapter 1
## Southern Lower Peninsula

# Peninsular Paper Company

Location:
Peninsular Park
1249 Leforge Road
Ypsilanti, MI 48198
42.25701857, -83.62467573

The Huron River, a vital waterway in southeast Michigan, meanders through the landscape, cascading over several dams to generate hydroelectric power before emptying into Lake Erie. One such dam, located just north of Eastern Michigan University's campus, once powered a significant industrial enterprise.

Perched on the north end of the dam, the remnants of the Peninsular Paper Company's powerhouse stands as a relic of the 19th-century industrial era. Constructed in 1867, this facility was built to supply paper to the Chicago Tribune. The strategic decision to source paper from a distant location was driven by the newspaper's desire to ensure a reliable supply, safeguarding against potential disruptions such as fires that could cripple a single supplier.

Unfortunately, the Peninsular Paper Mill suffered a devastating fire in 1873, forcing the Chicago Tribune to cancel its contract. Despite this setback, the company continued to operate, supplying paper to other customers until 2001.

Today, the old paper mill on the south side of the dam has been replaced by modern apartment complexes. The north side, however, remains a historical site, preserved as Peninsular Park. The abandoned powerhouse, a testament to the area's industrial past, is accessible to visitors who wish to explore its decaying interior.

Just a stone's throw from Peninsular Park, Depot Town in Ypsilanti offers a delightful mix of culinary delights and historical charm. Its vibrant streets are lined with inviting restaurants and lively bars, while the historic train depot, a relic of the town's railroad past, stands as a testament to its rich heritage.

# Eloise Asylum

Location:
30712 Michigan Avenue
Westland, MI 48185
42.28707929, -83.34263688

The Eloise Asylum, located in Westland on Michigan Avenue, is often whispered about as one of Michigan's most haunted places. While I can't confirm this claim, I can tell you that it was once the state's largest hospital and sanitarium. Though much of it has been lost to time, the remaining structures hold a peculiar, haunting beauty that invites speculation about its past and its alleged paranormal activity.

The land where these remnants stand began its history in 1939 when the Black Horse Tavern and its property were transformed into a poorhouse. To alleviate overcrowding at the Wayne County Poorhouse in Hamtramck, 35 needy residents were transferred to the newly constructed buildings. For years, it was known as the Wayne County Poorhouse until 1894 when a post office was established and named after Eloise Dickerson Davock, the daughter of Detroit's postmaster.

By 1913, the complex had grown into three distinct divisions: the Eloise Hospital (Mental Hospital), the Eloise Infirmary (Poorhouse), and the Eloise Sanitarium (T.B. Hospital). At its peak during the Great Depression, the complex housed an estimated 10,000 residents. It was a self-sufficient community, complete with its own police and fire departments, railroad and trolley stations, bakery, amusement hall, laundries, powerhouse, and extensive farming operations.

Dr. Albarran, a pioneer in medical technology, worked at Eloise and was among the first to utilize X-rays. Patients from Detroit and surrounding areas sought his expertise to gain a glimpse inside their bodies. Additionally, Eloise housed the state's first kidney dialysis unit and was a forerunner in the field of Music Therapy.

A stark reminder of the complex's past is its numerous cemeteries. With a population of 10,000, death was a frequent occurrence. Bodies were interred in various locations, one of which is a field marked by small stone markers bearing only numbers. The impersonal nature of these markers, lacking even a name, is a poignant testament to the harsh realities of the past. These cemeteries were used until 1948, after which a law was enacted to utilize bodies for medical training.

The farm operations ceased in 1958, followed by the closure of large psychiatric buildings in 1973. The state of Michigan took over the psychiatric division in 1977, leading to its gradual closure. The general hospital followed suit in 1984. Many buildings have been demolished, and the land has been repurposed for a golf course and condominiums. A Michigan Historical Marker stands near the parking lot, and the main building remains vacant, currently listed for sale.

The hospital's dark history and eerie atmosphere have made it a popular location for filmmakers. In 2017, it served as the backdrop for the horror film "Eloise," directed by Robert Legato. This fictionalized account, inspired by the hospital's real-life history, is sure to fuel the rumors and legends surrounding this enigmatic place.

In 2018, John Hambrick purchased the Eloise complex and has been transforming it into a haunted attraction. He is also in the process of adding a restaurant and a speakeasy to the site. The historic property offers tours for history enthusiasts and nighttime visits for paranormal investigators. If you're curious about taking a tour, be sure to visit their website at www.eloiseasylum.com

Located about a quarter mile south of Eloise on Henry Ruff Rd, the old asylum cemetery contains hundreds of graves marked solely by numbers.

# The Old State Prison

Location:
100 Armory Court.
Jackson, MI 49202
42.257647100, -84.406663384

The state's first penitentiary was established in 1838 near Jackson, Michigan. Initially a simple wooden structure, the prison quickly expanded to accommodate its growing inmate population. By 1839, it held thirty-five prisoners.

The early facility, resembling a fur trader's outpost, consisted of three log cabins surrounded by a crude wooden wall.

Because of its rudimentary design, escapes were frequent. In 1840, ten prisoners broke out and formed the notorious "Jackson Robber Gang," terrorizing the local community with a series of robberies. The Civil War further strained the prison's resources, leading to overcrowding and deteriorating conditions.

Under the brutal regime of Warden John Morris (1870-1875), inmates endured horrific abuse. One prisoner was whipped sixty-three times, while another's arm was permanently damaged by cruel restraints. Morris's cruelty was eventually exposed, leading to his prosecution.

In the late 19th century, a shift towards rehabilitation and education took place under Warden H. F. Hatch. Female inmates, who were initially housed with male prisoners, were eventually separated. One notable case was Sarah Havilland, a woman convicted of poisoning her children. Inside the prison, she became a caretaker for the warden's children.

By the early 20th century, the prison had become the states largest walled facility. However, overcrowding and violence remained persistent issues. A major riot erupted in 1912, highlighting the dire conditions within the prison.

In 1928, a new prison was built north of Jackson, and the old facility was closed in 1934. Despite numerous expansions over the years, the prison had always struggled to accommodate its growing population.

The stone walls with guard towers of the old prison still stand in Jackson. The old prison is now Armory Arts Village, a community of galleries, workspaces, and apartments. Adventure seekers can tour  the prison including the underground solitary confinement cells. Info on the tours can be found at www.historicprisontours.com

# Jeepers Creepers School

Location:
Intersection of W. Southern Rd.
and S. Snow Prairie Rd.
South of Coldwater
41.78248924, -85.1373113

The old schoolhouse south of Coldwater, a relic of the early 1900s, stands as a silent sentinel of a tragic past. Once filled with the sounds of youthful laughter and the pursuit of knowledge, its halls now echo with a different kind of history.

12

In the spring of 1990, a dark cloud descended upon the peaceful community. Marilyn DePue, a dedicated counselor at Coldwater High School, fell victim to a brutal domestic dispute. Her estranged husband, Dennis DePue, committed a horrific act of violence, taking her life. He dumped her body behind an old church, that has since been demolished, then drove extremely fast down South Snow Prairie Road, passing a brother and sister out on an afternoon drive. When the pair of siblings drove past the old school they noticed the van that had passed them. The two also saw a man hiding a bloody sheet behind the abandoned building. De Pue must have realized there was a blood soaked sheet in the van that he needed to hide.

The case, featured on the television show "Unsolved Mysteries," captivated the nation. Despite extensive efforts, DePue evaded capture, eventually taking his own life.

The chilling details of Marilyn DePue's murder have drawn eerie parallels to the opening scene of the horror film "Jeepers Creepers," though the filmmakers have denied any direct inspiration.

Today, the abandoned schoolhouse remains a haunting reminder of this tragic event. Its decaying structure stands in stark contrast to the serene rural landscape. As you drive past, you may feel a sense of unease, a silent acknowledgment of the darkness that once touched its grounds. The old school is privately owned and off limits to people.

You can get a good glimpse of the old school from the road but please be respectful and do not trespass since it is privately owned

# Fort Wayne

Location:
6325 W. Jefferson Avenue
Detroit, MI 48209
42.300938, -83.09530066

Fort Wayne, a historic landmark nestled along the Detroit River, stands as a testament to America's evolving military history. Constructed in the 19th century to safeguard the nation's northern border, the fort has played a crucial role in numerous conflicts and eras.

Originally built as a defensive stronghold, the fort served as a training ground for Union soldiers during the Civil War. Its strategic location and robust infrastructure made it a vital hub for military operations throughout the 20th century. During World Wars I and II, it facilitated the distribution of essential war supplies produced in the nearby industrial heartland. In the Cold War era, the fort's significance was renewed as it became part of a missile defense system designed to protect Detroit, a city critical to the nation's industrial might.

Today, the fort's imposing stone walls and remnants of its past offer a glimpse into America's military heritage. The Historic Fort Wayne Coalition, a dedicated nonprofit organization, is working tirelessly to preserve and restore this historic site. Visitors can explore the fort's grounds, marvel at its architecture, and learn about its rich history.

Yet, the fort's legacy extends beyond its tangible structures. Local folklore whispers of ghostly encounters, particularly within the eerie confines of the old tunnel. Tales of spectral soldiers, a chilling reminder of the fort's past, continue to intrigue and fascinate. While these stories may be rooted in legend, they add a layer of mystery to the fort's already captivating history.

The fort was abandoned by the military and many of the buildings are slowly crumbling. The coalition is working on stabilizing the fort and its buildings. During the summer months they offer guided tours of the grounds. It is a great way to see this historic property and learn about the fort's history.

# Dyer Kiln Ruins

Location:
8610 Sand Road
Bellevue, MI 49021
42.44226620, -85.02932463

West of Bellevue, located within a quiet county park along Sand Road, lies a forgotten relic of Michigan's industrial past: the Dyer Kiln. This crumbling stone structure, once a bustling hub of activity, played a crucial role in the construction of the state Capitol building in Lansing.

Built in 1880 by Thomas Roberts, the kiln was used to burn limestone into lime, a key ingredient in mortar. The resulting lime was transported to Lansing, where it was used to bind the bricks and stones of the majestic Capitol building.

After nearly two decades of operation, the kiln fell silent in 1899, its purpose fulfilled. The surrounding land was later transformed into a small park called Dyer Kiln Park, preserving this historical site for future generations. Today, visitors can see the kiln's ruins, imagining the heat and toil of its bygone era.

# Meads Mill Ruins

Location:
Hines Park
11400 Edward N Hines Drive
Plymouth, MI 48170
42.4030946, -83.4705115

Hines Park is a Wayne County park situated between Northville and Plymouth. The Middle River Rouge flows through it and you may notice an old stone structure that crosses the river. A nearby sign reads Meads Mill. It was built in 1830 and at the time was the largest flour mill in the state of Michigan. The mill burned down in 1857 and was never rebuilt.

Even though the sign near the ruins reads Meads Mill, from what I have found, it is believed that the current ruins were part of a 1937 Works Progress Administration project. The stones were the foundation of a waterwheel and intake site for the Wayne County Training School powerhouse. Whatever the ruins were for, it is an interesting place to visit with a nice little waterfall.

# The Ruins At Haven Hill

Location:
Haven Road
Highland State Recreation Area
White Lake, MI 48383
42.6411036, -83.5634134

In the heart of Oakland County, nestled amidst rolling hills and serene forests is the Highland Recreation Area. Inside its boundaries lies the remnants of a bygone era. Haven Hill, once a luxurious retreat for the Ford family and their illustrious guests, now stands as a haunting reminder of its former glory.

Edsel Ford, son of automotive pioneer Henry Ford, purchased the land in the early 1920s. On this picturesque property, he constructed a massive log lodge, a haven for relaxation and entertainment. The estate, which included a carriage house, pool, stables, tennis courts, and a toboggan run, was a popular destination for the Ford family and their famous friends, such as Thomas Edison, Charles Lindbergh, and Jackie Cooper.

Haven Hill Lodge Before the fire.

After Edsel Ford's passing in 1943, the estate was acquired by the state of Michigan and transformed into a state park. However, due to budget cuts, the park's visitor centers, including the historic lodge, were forced to close. Tragically, the lodge was destroyed by arson in 1999.

Today, visitors can still explore the grounds of Haven Hill, though the once-grand lodge is gone. The remaining foundations, stonework, and a portion of the chimney offer a glimpse into its former splendor. Circular markers indicate the locations of various rooms, allowing visitors to imagine the layout and grandeur of the estate. Other structures, such as the carriage house, still stand, offering a tangible connection to the past.

As you wander through the ruins, you can't help but feel a sense of nostalgia and wonder. Haven Hill, once a symbol of wealth and privilege, now serves as a poignant reminder of the passage of time and the impermanence of human endeavors.

# Maybury's Abandoned Cars

Location:
Maybury State Park
49601 Eight Mile W,
Northville, MI 48167
42.42552, -83.52855

Deep within the woods of Maybury State Park west of Northville, a pair of dilapidated cars remain as silent witnesses to a bygone era. One, overturned and skeletal, barely resembles a vehicle. The other, upright but stripped of its parts, stands as a haunting reminder of decay.

The park's history is as intriguing as its eerie relics. Once a bustling hub, the Maybury Sanatorium opened its doors in 1919. A self-contained city, it boasted 40 buildings and its own power plant. However, as medical advancements rendered its services obsolete, the sanitarium closed in 1969. By 1975, most of its structures had been demolished. The State of Michigan Department of Natural Resources then acquired the land, transforming it into the serene Maybury State Park we know today.

The cars would be difficult to remove so I guess it was determined it would be best for them to stay where they are near the mountain bike trail. Not much remains of the sanitarium but a few foundations and some old roads.

> The cars are located off the mountain bike trail. You can take the paved bike trail to emergency post number 29. The cars are about 50 yards into the woods from there.

# Chapter 2
# Central Lower Peninsula

# Mount Pleasant Indian Industrial Boarding School

Location:
South Crawford Road near West Pickard Road. This is on tribal property where no trespassing is allowed and is strictly enforced, but you can get a good view of the buildings from South Crawford Road.
43.6151917, -84.78798056

In the late 19th century, the United States government embarked on a systematic effort to assimilate Native American tribes into American culture. This policy, often driven by religious zeal and a desire to exploit Native lands, resulted in the forced removal of children from their families and communities.

One such institution was the Mount Pleasant Indian Industrial Boarding School, established in 1892. This school, like many others across the country, was designed to strip Native American children of their cultural identity and replace it with Euro-American values and norms. Enrollment had increased significantly and it was necessary to build additional buildings to house all of the students and their daily activities. These included separate boys and girls dormitories, a hospital, a woodworking and blacksmith shop, a building for industrial training, a dining hall, a clubhouse for the employees of the school, and several farm buildings. Students were subjected to harsh discipline, physical and emotional abuse, and often endured poor living conditions. Tragically, at least 174 children died while attending the school, their deaths largely undocumented.

The school closed in 1934 and was repurposed as a facility for individuals with mental disabilities. This subsequent use, coupled with the school's dark history, has led to rumors of haunting and paranormal activity. While the property is now privately owned and closely monitored, remnants of the past, including several historic buildings, can still be seen on South Crawford Road near Mission Creek Woodland Park. It's important to remember the painful legacy of these institutions and to honor the memory of the Native American children who suffered and died.

If you drive past the old buildings, please be respectful and do not trespass. The buildings are on tribal property and are under constant surveillance.

# Port Hope Chimney

Location:
Stafford County Park
8421 State Street,
Port Hope, MI 48468
43.94392021, -82.70899069

The imposing brick structure looming over Port Hope, Michigan, initially resembles a lighthouse due to its proximity to Lake Huron. However, a closer look reveals its true identity, thanks to a nearby historical marker.

31

This towering remnant, now nestled within Stafford County Park, is all that remains of the once-thriving sawmills that powered Port Hope's economy. Erected in 1858 by local mason John Geitz, the chimney was commissioned by lumberman William R. Stafford. Stafford, along with his partner William Southard, acquired federal land in the area, originally designated for veterans' pensions, to fuel their lumbering operations.

The sawmill and the town of Port Hope flourished hand-in-hand. However, the Great Fire of 1871 ravaged the town and sawmill, though they were eventually rebuilt. A decade later, another devastating fire consumed the sawmill and much of the region's timber. Undeterred, Stafford pivoted his business, constructing a flour mill and a dock extending into Lake Huron. Port Hope continued to serve the surrounding agricultural community, with ships carrying wheat and grain to and from the town's harbor.

While the town has evolved over time, the enduring brick chimney stands as a testament to the region's lumbering heritage, offering a glimpse into the past and a reminder of the industry that once shaped the Thumb.

Just a few miles north of Port Hope, you'll find the historic Pointe Aux Barques Lighthouse and Life Saving Station.

# Tyrone Sunken Gardens

Location:
In the Back of Tyrone Memory
Gardens Cemetery
10260 White Lake Rd.
Fenton, Michigan 48430
42.7690130, -83.759488

Located behind the serene Tyrone Memory Gardens Cemetery, a unique and mysterious stone monument awaits discovery. This hidden gem, known as the Tyrone Sunken Gardens, is a testament to the vision and wanderlust of Charles Eugene Smith.

Smith, a world traveler, was inspired by the famous rock gardens of Iceland and the sunken gardens of London and Mexico City. In 1930, he embarked on a project to create his own tranquil oasis in Fenton, Michigan. The result is a captivating arrangement of stones from each state and bearing its state motto and flower.

Carved into a large stone at the entrance, Smith's inscription provides a glimpse into his global adventures and his desire to share his experiences:

"After having traveled around the world four different times and visited parts of Europe, Asia, North America, South America, North and South Africa, Australia and the islands of New Zealand, Tasmania, St. Helena, Canary, Fiji, Ceylon, Iceland, Hawaii, Philippines, New Foundland, Faeroe and many others and considering the famous rock gardens of Iceland and the sunken gardens of London, England, and Mexico City the most beautiful I contribute this memorial in my memory to this small garden."

The stones, some dating back to the 1700s, are meticulously placed in a circular pattern, once surrounding a sundial. The garden's serene atmosphere, coupled with the intriguing history and inspiring quotes, makes it a truly special place.

Though the exact details of Smith's life remain a mystery, his legacy lives on in the Sunken Gardens. This hidden treasure offers a peaceful retreat and a reminder of the world's beauty and diversity.

The beautiful sculptures in the cemetery were created by artist and sculptor Robert St. Croix.

# Spartan: The Other Sister

Location:
701 Maritime Drive
Ludington, MI 49431
43.948588, -86.4504661

The iconic *S.S. Badger*, a historic car ferry, continues to ply the waters of Lake Michigan, traversing the route between Ludington, Michigan, and Manitowoc, Wisconsin. Her twin, the *S.S. Spartan*, remains moored in Ludington, a silent sentinel of the past.

Both vessels were constructed in 1950 by the C&O Railroad. While the railroad typically named its ferries after cities, the *Spartan* and *Badger* were chosen to honor the mascots of Michigan State University and the University of Wisconsin, respectively.

By the late 1970s, declining ferry service led to plans to lease the Spartan to the Ann Arbor Railroad for operations out of Frankfort. However, the harbor's shallow depth made this impractical. Since 1980, the *Spartan* has been tied up in Ludington, serving as a valuable source of spare parts for the *Badger*.

The *Badger* holds the distinction of being a National Historic Landmark, recognized by the National Park Service. This unique designation highlights its significance as a mobile historical site, joining the ranks of iconic landmarks like the San Francisco cable cars.

Next time you visit Ludington. Check out the abandoned *S.S. Spartan* at the end of Maritime Drive where the *Badger* is loaded with vehicles. The *Spartan* sits there, patiently awaiting its sister's return when it is gone. It also stands at the ready with donor parts to keep the historic *Badger* in operation.

# Lincoln Brick Factory Ruins

Location:
13991 Tallman Road
Grand Ledge, MI 48837
42.7692673, -84.76492792

The Grand River, winding its way through the town of Grand Ledge, Michigan, has played a significant role in shaping the area's history. The river's fertile banks were home to abundant clay deposits, a resource that Native Americans utilized for pottery-making. Later, these clay deposits would become the foundation for a thriving brick industry.

In 1914, the Baker Clay Company established a factory along the river, pioneering the use of a continuous kiln in the United States. This innovative technology, adapted from Canadian designs, significantly increased production efficiency. Initially producing glazed clay tiles for farm silos, the company shifted its focus to bricks as concrete gained popularity in silo construction.

Rebranded as the Grand Ledge Face Brick Company, the factory produced millions of bricks, many of which contributed to the construction of iconic buildings across Michigan, including structures at Michigan State University, such as Beaumont Tower.

The factory's operations continued until 1947, when it was acquired by the Lincoln Brick Factory. In 1975, Eaton County purchased the property and transformed it into Lincoln Brick Park. Today, some of the walls are still standing and visitors can explore the remnants of the old factory.

Another nearby Eaton County park, Fitzgerald Park, boasts stunning hiking trails along the Grand River and a historic barn-style theater that was once a gathering place for Spiritualists.

# Grand Haven Coal Tipple

Location:
301 N Harbor Dr,
Grand Haven, MI 49417
43.06768882, -86.2301799

Looming over the picturesque town of Grand Haven, Michigan, stands a colossal concrete structure: a relic of the bygone era of steam locomotives. This imposing coal tipple once served as a vital link in the Grand Trunk

Western Railroad's network, fueling the powerful steam engines that hauled freight and passengers across the region.

During the heyday of rail travel, Grand Haven was a bustling hub, with ferry service transporting rail cars across Lake Michigan. The coal tipple played a crucial role in keeping these trains moving, efficiently transferring coal from storage to the hungry locomotives. However, as the railroad industry transitioned to diesel power in the 1950s, the tipple's purpose became obsolete.

The decline of rail traffic in the 1970s led to the abandonment of the Grand Trunk's Grand Haven rail yard. Fortunately, this industrial relic has been preserved and transformed into a public park. Today, visitors can marvel at the towering tipple and explore the historic railway equipment on display, including the iconic Pere Marquette 1223 steam locomotive. This fascinating piece of railroad history offers a glimpse into the past and a reminder of the vital role that trains played in shaping the region.

# The Old Factory in Newaygo

Across from Riverfront Park
85 E Water St,
Newaygo, MI 49337
43.423379213, -85.7996122

The central Michigan town of Newaygo, sits on the banks of the Muskegon River at the southern edge of the Manistee National Forest, holds a fascinating piece of industrial history. A visit to the riverfront park, situated between the old train bridge and the M-37 bridge, reveals remnants of the once-thriving Henry Rowe Manufacturing Company.

In the early 1900s, Joseph Henry Rowe, a prominent businessman in Newaygo, established this factory to produce a variety of wooden products, including tools, furniture components, and architectural trim. The factory's strategic location along the Muskegon River allowed for efficient transportation of goods, while the powerful Penoyer Creek provided the necessary water power to operate the machinery.

Today, the ruins of the factory stand as a testament to the area's industrial past. The small waterfall, cascading from a man-made trough into the Muskegon River, is a reminder of the creek's role in powering the factory. While the factory itself is long gone, its legacy lives on in the history of Newaygo and the surrounding region.

Nearby, the Croton and Hardy Dams offer interesting sights. You can even drive over Hardy Dam and view old generator parts in the adjacent park.

# Port Huron Railroad Dock

Location:
100 Wall St Vl,
Port Huron, MI 48060
42.96977778, -82.42047976

Located along the River Walk near downtown Port
Huron, a peculiar structure stands as a silent testament to
the region's industrial past. This once-bustling dock,
constructed in 1903, served as a vital link in the rail
network, ferrying rail cars across the St. Clair River to
Canada.

45

For three decades, the ferry chugged along, carrying heavy loads of goods until the Great Depression forced its operations to cease in 1933. Decades later, in 1950, the dock was revived to accommodate the increased rail traffic between Dow Chemical's plants in Midland and Sarnia.

However, as transportation methods evolved, the ferry's services were no longer required, leading to its final retirement in 1994. The dock, once a bustling hub of activity, was left to the elements, slowly decaying into obscurity.

In 2013, the Community Foundation breathed new life into the historic structure, refurbishing it into a scenic platform to admire the majestic ships gliding down the St. Clair River. Today, this forgotten relic offers a unique glimpse into the industrial heritage of the region, inviting visitors to ponder the bygone era of riverine transportation.

The Great Lakes Maritime Center, situated nearby, houses a museum and provides an excellent vantage point for observing freighter traffic. Although Michigan's easternmost point is technically a few hundred yards north on private industrial land, the center offers a close approximation.

# Chapter 3
# Northern Lower Peninsula

# Grousehaven Lodge

Location:
Rifle River Recreation Area
2550 Rose City Road,
Lupton, MI 48635
44.40736160, -84.01012790

Hidden within the Rifle River Recreation Area, near the
towering Jewett Observation Tower, lies a relic of the
past: the remnants of the once-grand Grousehaven
Lodge. All that remains is an old basement or wine cellar,
a secret waiting to be discovered. Look for the guardrail in

the parking area south of the tower; the cellar lies beneath. Venture down the hill, and you'll find the entrance to this historical hideaway.

The man behind this luxurious retreat was Harry Mulford "Hal" Jewett, a legendary athlete from the late 19th century. A Notre Dame star, he set records in the 220-yard dash and triple jump, and even scored the school's first-ever touchdown against the University of Michigan. After his athletic career, Jewett became a successful businessman, eventually serving as president of the Paige Motor Car Company.

In the 1920s, Jewett's love for the outdoors led him to purchase 7,000 acres of land near Lupton. With the help of skilled Finnish axemen and Detroit-area workers, he constructed a magnificent two-story log lodge, complete with modern amenities like steam heat, electricity, and a stunning observation room. Grousehaven became a world-class hunting preserve, renowned for its abundant game, including ruffed grouse, partridge, and pheasant. Jewett also worked to improve the local fishing, stocking the Rifle River with trout.

Tragically, Jewett's life was cut short in 1933. His heirs, losing interest in the property, sold it to the state of Michigan in 1945. The lodge was eventually demolished in 1967, leaving behind only fragments of its former glory. Today, the hidden cellar is a reminder of Jewett's legacy and the grandeur of Grousehaven.

> Visitors can drive up to the lookout tower. It is located on Ridge Road, a one way dirt road that starts near the entrance.

# Wreck Of The Joseph S. Fay

Location:
7323 U.S. Highway 23,
Rogers City, 49779
The wreck lies on the shoreline
in front of the 40 Mile Point
Lighthouse
45.486848310, -83.9143026

The wreckage of the *J.S. Fay*, a wooden steamship that once plied the Great Lakes, offers a unique opportunity to witness maritime history firsthand. Unlike most shipwrecks, which remain submerged beneath the waves, the remains of the *Fay* are exposed on the shores of Lake Huron.

The night of October 19, 1905, was a stormy one. The *Fay*, towing another vessel, the *Rhodes*, was caught in a violent storm. The captain, seeking shelter from the raging waves, hugged the coast, but the wind shifted, straining the towline until it snapped, taking a piece of the *Fay*'s stern with it.

Water poured into the hull, forcing the crew to huddle in the forward cabin. The captain, determined to reach shore, steered the ship toward the 40 Mile Point Light Station. The bow struck a sandbar, and the force of the waves ripped off the entire forward cabin, including the wheelhouse and captain's room. Miraculously, these structures were carried ashore, saving the lives of the captain and ten crew members.

However, not everyone was as fortunate. First Mate David Syze and two other crew members were forced to cling to the wrecked hull. Desperate to reach shore, they fashioned a makeshift paddle from a spar. While two of the men made it safely, Syze, weakened by the cold, was lost to the unforgiving lake.

The *J.S. Fay's* tragic end is a stark reminder of the dangers faced by Great Lakes mariners. Its exposed wreckage serves as a poignant memorial to those who lost their lives and a testament to the power of nature. The timbers of the hull can still be seen in the sands of the shoreline. The level of the water in Lake Huron determines how much of the timbers can be seen. It is a short walk to the wreckage from the lighthouse. A sign points visitors in the right direction.

In addition to the lighthouse, the park is home to the wheelhouse of the first *Calcite* freighter.

# Cheboygan Lighthouse Ruins

Location:
Cheboygan State Park
4490 Beach Road,
Cheboygan, MI 49721
45.66894271, -84.41978244

The remnants of the Cheboygan Point Lighthouse, a historic beacon that once guided ships through the Straits of Mackinac, can be found along the shores of Lake Huron in Cheboygan State Park.

The first lighthouse at Cheboygan Point was constructed in 1851. It consisted of a dwelling and a 40-foot round brick tower equipped with a Fifth Order Fresnel lens. However, due to erosion, the tower was removed after only eight years of service.

In 1859, a new lighthouse was built, featuring an eight-foot square wooden tower atop a two-story dwelling. This lighthouse remained in operation until 1930, when the construction of the Fourteen Foot Shoal Light rendered it obsolete. The land was then deeded to the State of Michigan, and the buildings were eventually dismantled. Today, only the foundation remains, a silent testament to the lighthouse's past.

The Cheboygan Point Lighthouse also marked the entrance to Duncan Bay and Duncan City, a once-thriving community. As the county seat of Cheboygan County from 1853 to 1857, Duncan City served as a lumbering hub and a refueling stop for Great Lakes steamships. However, as the Cheboygan River was dredged deeper, allowing for increased shipping traffic, Duncan City's importance dwindled. The final blow came in 1898 when a devastating fire destroyed the town's sawmill. Today, only remnants of Duncan City remain, scattered across the landscape.

The green or the blue trail will take hikers to the ruins of the old lighthouse. At the beach near the lighthouse the Fourteen Foot Shoals Light can be seen offshore.

# Bell Ghost Town

Location:
Besser Natural Area on Besser
Bell Road near
12057 E Grand Lake Rd.
Presque Isle, MI 49777
45.2451657, -83.4144914

Jesse Besser, a visionary entrepreneur, revolutionized the concrete block industry in the early 20th century. His innovative methods led to the creation of one of the largest block companies in the United States. Before his passing, Besser generously donated a vast tract of land along Lake Huron, north of Alpena, for public enjoyment. This land now forms the picturesque Besser Natural Area, a haven for hikers seeking solitude and natural beauty.

As you wander along the one-mile loop trail, you'll encounter the intriguing remnants of the forgotten town of Bell. A towering stone chimney marks the site of this once-bustling logging community. Nearby, you'll find the crumbling walls of an old general store and a broken safe, silent witnesses to the town's past. The ground is littered with artifacts, such as bits of metal and antique cans, offering a glimpse into the lives of the people who once called Bell home. It's important to remember to leave these historical artifacts in place for future visitors to discover.

The village of Bell grew alongside the Presque Isle Brick and Lumber Company. In 1884, a post office was established, likely operating within the general store. However, as the town's fortunes waned, the post office closed its doors in 1911. When visiting the area, be prepared for a potential encounter with the local insect population, particularly during the spring months.

In addition to the hiking loop, a trail leads south to the Rockport State Recreation Area. A short distance along this trail, you'll discover the unique Bell Pines Clubhouse. Constructed by the Besser Corporation using their innovative concrete block technology, this distinctive building remains privately owned and is used for various events.

The old Bell Cemetery lies west of the parking lot. A two-track near the power lines leads to the historic cemetery.

# Alligator Hill Kilns

Location:
Off of Stocking Road
Empire, MI 49630
44.88955090, -86.0217346

The Sleeping Bear Dunes National Lakeshore, a breathtaking expanse of pristine coastline along Lake Michigan, offers a diverse range of outdoor activities. From scaling towering sand dunes to exploring historic sites, there's something for everyone. One such historical site, tucked away near the Alligator Hill hiking trail, is a series of intriguing concrete structures.

These concrete kilns, constructed in the 1950s by lumberman Pierce Stocking, played a vital role in the local economy. Stocking's sawmill, located near Alligator Hill, generated a significant amount of wood waste. To maximize the use of this resource, he devised a plan to convert the waste into charcoal. The charcoal was then packaged and sold to stores throughout Michigan for barbecue grills.

The kilns themselves are fascinating structures. Wood waste, such as limbs and slabs, was tightly packed inside the concrete ovens. The open front was sealed with concrete blocks, and a fire was ignited just before the final blocks were set in place. The art of controlling the fire was delicate; too much air would consume the wood too quickly, while too little would suffocate the flames. If the process was successful, the wood would smolder slowly for several days, gradually transforming into charcoal. Once the fire had extinguished, the charcoal was removed, cooled, and then bagged for distribution. Visitors to the site can explore the old kilns and some of the walls are still black from the charcoal making process.

Nearby is D.H. Day's historic barn. It is probably the most photographed barn in Michigan.

# Deward Ghost Town

Location:
Off N. Manistee River Rd.
Frederic, MI 49733
44.836173, -84.836904

The ghost town of Deward, a testament to Michigan's lumbering past, owes its existence to the legacy of David E. Ward, a prominent lumber baron. Upon his death in 1900, Ward's will stipulated that his vast timberlands be liquidated within twelve years. To accomplish this task, his

65

sons constructed a massive sawmill along the Manistee River, northwest of Grayling. As the mill drew workers from far and wide, a bustling town emerged, named "Deward" after the "D. WARD" painted on the side of the mill.

Deward quickly grew into a thriving community, boasting a population of over 800 residents. Boarding houses, a general store, a church, and a community center catered to the needs of the lumberjacks and their families. The town's unique character was shaped by its prohibition of alcohol, reflecting the temperance movement of the time. For twelve intense years, the sawmill operated at full

capacity, devouring the region's vast forests. Once the timber was depleted, the town's purpose was fulfilled. The sawmill ceased operations in 1912, and Deward gradually faded into obscurity. Buildings were dismantled and hauled away, and the once-mighty sawmill was reduced to rubble.

Today, all that remains of Deward are a few concrete foundations, scattered amidst the forest. To reach these remnants of the past, follow County Road 612 north of West Cameron Bridge Road. A small green sign with a binoculars symbol marks the turnoff to a two-track road. Follow this road for about 100 yards to a parking area. From there, a trail leads down to the river, where you'll encounter the remnants of the sawmill's concrete foundations. These massive structures, adorned with large threaded rods, offer a glimpse into the industrial might of a bygone era.

> While the road to Deward is accessible by car during the summer months, a truck or SUV is recommended, especially during the wet spring and fall seasons.

# The Ruins in Onaway

Location:
Awakon Park
21121 M-68
Onaway, MI 49765
45.3550327, -84.23676190

The quiet town of Onaway, located south of Black Lake, holds a fascinating piece of industrial history. Within the boundaries of the newly established Awakon Park, visitors will encounter the remnants of the American Wood Rim Company, a once-thriving enterprise that played a significant role in the early days of the automobile industry.

68

Founded in 1901 by Edward J. Lobdell, the company capitalized on the abundant maple forests surrounding Onaway to produce high-quality bicycle rims. By 1905, the company had captured a remarkable 65% of the global bicycle rim market.

As the automobile industry gained momentum, the company pivoted to manufacturing wooden steering wheels. The complex, sprawling across over 44 acres, included the Lobdell-Emery Manufacturing Company, which oversaw the sawmill operations and produced a variety of wood products, such as broom handles and shingles.

At its peak, the American Wood Rim Company employed 1,200 workers and supplied steering wheels to nearly every major automobile manufacturer, except for Ford, which produced its own. The company's influence extended beyond the automotive industry, providing steering wheels for boats, airplanes, and tractors.

However, tragedy struck in June 1926 when a fire erupted in the sander building, quickly spreading throughout the complex and claiming the lives of four workers. The devastating fire crippled the company's operations, leaving a significant shortage of steering wheels for the burgeoning automobile industry. To mitigate the crisis, Lobdell purchased the vacant Republic Truck plant in Alma, and over 300 workers relocated to continue production. This event marked a turning point for Onaway, as many residents followed the jobs to Alma, leaving the town to decline.

Today, Awakon Park offers a glimpse into this forgotten chapter of industrial history. A half-mile trail winds through the former factory site, where visitors can still see the concrete foundations and remnants of the once-bustling complex. Informative signage provides insights into the company's history and its impact on the local community.

The park also contains several metal sculptures created by Tom Moran. A native of Onaway, Michigan, after graduating high school, he founded Moran Iron Works, a company specializing in large-scale metal fabrication. The company operates in Onaway and Rogers City. He has created many ornamental metal artworks that can be seen around the state.

# Durant Castle

Location:
Located in the Mason Tract
Off Mason Tract Trail Rd.
44.5638650, -84.50678381

Hidden deep within the forests of the Mason Tract, northeast of Roscommon, lies the haunting remnant of a bygone era: the foundation of a grand mansion, once envisioned as a secluded retreat. This opulent structure was the dream of Russell Clifford Durant, son of the legendary William C. Durant, founder of General Motors.

In the late 1920s, Durant embarked on the construction of a 54-room mansion, a testament to his wealth and ambition. The castle-like structure was designed to offer breathtaking views of the surrounding wilderness, particularly the South Branch of the Au Sable River. However, fate had other plans. Before the Durants could ever call the mansion home, tragedy struck. In 1931, a fire, believed to have been caused by carelessly discarded turpentine-soaked rags, engulfed the nearly completed structure. The Great Depression further dampened the

Durants' spirits, leading them to abandon plans for rebuilding.

Over time, the ruins of the mansion slowly succumbed to nature's relentless forces. The once-grand structure was dismantled, leaving behind only the foundations. Today, the site serves as a serene picnic area within the Mason Tract. While little remains of the mansion itself, exploring the overgrown foundation offers a glimpse into the past and a reminder of the fleeting nature of human endeavors.

# Rockport

Location:
Old Grade Road
Alpena, MI 49707
45.20234490, -83.38416688

Rockport State Recreation Area is a unique gem among Michigan's state parks. While many others are known for their traditional camping, swimming, and hiking experiences, Rockport offers a distinctive blend of history, geology, and natural beauty.

Once a bustling stone quarry, the site operated from 1914 to the late 1950s. A deep harbor and a massive mechanical loading dock facilitated the shipment of stone, including crucial materials for the foundations of the Mackinac Bridge. After the quarry's closure, the buildings and worker housing were dismantled, leaving behind only the foundations of the loading dock, which still extends into the clear waters of Lake Huron.

The land was transferred to Consumers Power before being gifted to the Michigan Department of Natural Resources in the 1990s. In 2012, it officially became Michigan's 100th state park.

Today, visitors can explore the rugged landscape, discovering remnants of the quarry's industrial past along the hiking trails. A two-mile hike leads to several intriguing sinkholes. At night, the park's designation as a Dark Sky Park provides exceptional stargazing opportunities, with clear views of the Milky Way. If you're seeking a distinctive outdoor experience, consider visiting Rockport State Recreation Area, located north of Alpena on the sunrise side of the state.

Rockhounds can search for Petoskey stones and fossils, and while most state and federal lands prohibit rock removal, Rockport State Recreation Area allows visitors to collect up to 25 pounds per person per year.

# Frankfort Ironworks

Location:
Waterfront Park
1074 Furnace St,
Elberta, MI 49628
44.6269605, -86.23503949

These crumbling brick walls, nestled near the shores of Lake Michigan, offer a glimpse into Michigan's industrial past. The ruins of the Frankfort Iron Works, constructed in 1870, once hummed with activity as they smelted iron ore mined from the Upper Peninsula's Escanaba region. Despite the name, the ironworks are actually located in Elberta, across Betsie Lake from downtown Frankfort.

The ironworks relied on the abundant hardwood forests surrounding the area to fuel its furnaces. However, as the demand for fuel grew, the workers were forced to venture deeper into the Michigan wilderness to source firewood. By 1883, the limitations of fuel supply forced the ironworks to cease operations.

The railroad company acquired the site and repurposed it as a marine terminal for loading rail cars onto ferries. The buildings were converted into workshops and a roundhouse for locomotive maintenance. The terminal remained operational until 1982. Today, the site is part of Elberta's Waterfront Park.

While the ruins are fenced off to protect visitors from falling bricks, you can still get close enough to appreciate the scale and intricate details of the remaining structures. If you find yourself in the Frankfort area, it's well worth taking a short detour to explore this fascinating piece of Michigan's industrial heritage.

> The park is also home to an old U.S. Lifesaving Station. The old station is now used as a banquet hall.

# Empire Lumber Mill Ruins

Location:
Empire Beach
10484 Niagara St,
Empire, MI 49630
44.8118256, -86.067613

On sunny summer days, Lake Michigan's shores in Empire draw beachgoers to its sandy expanse. Amidst the playground's laughter, a curious sight emerges: a large concrete block topped with rusty metal rods. This relic is a testament to Empire's vibrant lumbering past.

79

The first mill, established by George Aylsworth between 1873 and 1883, marked the beginning. In 1885, Potter and Struthers built a second mill, later acquired by T. Wilce Company and renamed the Empire Lumber Company in 1887. This mill, one of the largest and most advanced in the region, was capable of producing a staggering twenty million board feet of lumber annually.

Tragedy struck twice, with devastating fires in 1906 and 1917. Though the mill was rebuilt after the first fire, the second proved fatal. With the region's virgin timber dwindling, the mill was not resurrected. Today, the concrete block stands as a poignant reminder of Empire's once-thriving lumber industry, inviting visitors to ponder the town's rich history.

# Udell Fire Tower

Location:
Fire Tower Road
Manistee, MI 49660
44.20860366, -86.10025035

Michigan once had a network of lookout towers, manned by rangers who scanned the forests for signs of fire. The Udell Lookout Tower, a 100-foot-tall structure built by the Civilian Conservation Corps (CCC) in 1936, is the only remaining lookout tower in the Lower Peninsula still standing on National Forest property.

Used until the 1960s, when airplanes took over fire spotting duties, the tower offers a glimpse into the past. Though the first set of stairs has been removed, making it inaccessible, the tower still stands as a testament to the hard work of the CCC and the vital role it played in forest conservation.

The old fire tower can be reached by taking Fire Tower Road from M-55.

# Francisco Morazan Wreckage

Location:
South Shore of
South Manitou Island
44.997600339, -86.14170799

The *SS Francisco Morazan*, a cargo ship constructed in Germany in 1922, had a storied history marked by numerous name changes and ownership transfers. Renamed in 1959, the Morazan departed Chicago on November 27, 1960, carrying cargo destined for the

Netherlands and Germany. However, a fierce storm forced the ship aground on South Manitou Island in Lake Michigan on November 28th. Fortunately, the crew was safely evacuated, but the ship was irreparably damaged.

Today, the wreck of the *Francisco Morazan* remains a haunting reminder of the past, visible from the shores of South Manitou Island. It has become a popular site for divers and snorkelers, offering a unique underwater experience and a glimpse into the maritime history of the Great Lakes. As part of the Manitou Passage State Underwater Preserve, the wreck is protected, ensuring its preservation for generations to come.

A ferry service to the Manitou Islands is operated from Fishtown in Leland.

# Antique Alley

Location:
Louis M. Groen Nature Preserve
10950 Heatherton Rd,
Johannesburg, MI 49751
44.9962306, -84.4576850

Deep within the sprawling 800-acre Louis M. Groen
Nature Preserve lies a captivating piece of history. The
remnants of the Johannesburg Manufacturing Company
and sawmill, including an antique windmill and decaying
wooden structures, stand as a testament to a bygone era.

This once-thriving industry, operational until 1929, produced over 300 million board feet of lumber and employed up to 200 people.

A unique attraction within the preserve is Antique Alley, a trail lined with rusting trucks and farming equipment from the old factory. These relics of the past, slowly succumbing to time's relentless march, offer a fascinating glimpse into the industrial history of the region.

Another historical gem is the Echo Valley Resort, a stone motel that has fallen silent. Though currently inaccessible to visitors, its imposing stone structure remains a striking sight.

Managed by Otsego County Parks, the preserve boasts well-marked trails that lead hikers past these intriguing abandoned sites. As you explore the serene natural beauty of the area, you'll encounter these remnants of the past, inviting you to ponder the stories they hold.

The preserve is named for Louis M. Groen, who once owned the property. After the deaths of both Groen and his wife, the land was generously donated to the county. Groen was a notable figure in the fast-food industry, owning several McDonald's franchises in Ohio and famously inventing the iconic Filet-O-Fish sandwich.

# Chapter 4
# Upper Peninsula

# Quincy Dredge Number 2

Location:
Torch Lake North of Hancock
on M-26
47.14510481, -88.4596354

If you find yourself traversing the scenic M-26 along the Keweenaw Peninsula, be sure to keep an eye out for a truly colossal sight: the Quincy Dredge. This massive, rusting metal behemoth, partially submerged in the waters of Torch Lake, is a testament to the region's rich mining history.

In the late 19th and early 20th centuries, the Keweenaw Peninsula was a hub of copper mining activity. As mining operations intensified, vast quantities of copper-bearing ore were processed in stamping mills. The resulting waste material, a fine copper-laden sand, was often discharged into nearby lakes and rivers.

To recover valuable copper from this discarded sand, innovative solutions were sought. The Calumet and Hecla Mining Company commissioned the construction of the dredge in 1914. This colossal machine was designed to scoop up the sand from the bottom of Torch Lake and transport it to the company's mill in Lake Linden for further processing.

Later acquired by the Quincy Mining Company, the dredge continued its work until 1967, when it sank during a winter layup. With the company facing financial difficulties, the decision was made to leave the dredge in its watery grave.

Today, the Quincy Dredge stands as a poignant reminder of the region's industrial past. Recognized as a historic site since 1978, it attracts visitors from far and wide who come to marvel at its sheer size and contemplate the stories it has to tell.

Across from the old dredge on M-26 is the abandoned Quincy Mining Company Stamp Mill #1

# Camp Raco

Location:
17998 M-28
Brimley, MI 49715
46.3672785, -84.73877428

During World War II, the serene landscapes of Michigan's Upper Peninsula were briefly disrupted by the presence of German prisoners of war. One such site was Camp Raco, located near Brimley.

93

Before becoming a POW camp, Camp Raco had a different purpose. In the 1930s, as part of President Roosevelt's New Deal, the Civilian Conservation Corps (CCC) established the camp. Hundreds of young men, primarily from Detroit, worked tirelessly to construct forest roads, bridges, and buildings in the surrounding area. Many of the state park structures in the region can be attributed to the CCC's efforts.

When the U.S. entered World War II, Camp Raco was reactivated to house German prisoners of war. Approximately 267 captured Nazi soldiers were confined within its walls.

Today, little remains of the camp. The buildings have been dismantled, leaving behind only stone foundations and a chimney. To glimpse this forgotten chapter of history, take a detour off M-28 near Brimley and follow the small wooden National Forest sign for Camp Raco. A short drive down a two-track road will lead you to the remnants of the camp, a silent testament to a bygone era.

> There were 32 POW Camps in Michigan with 6 in the Upper Peninsula.

# Fiborn Quarry

Location:
Fiborn Quarry Road about 3
miles north of Trout Lake Road
46.2060794, -85.1773706

Deep within the remote forests of Michigan's Upper
Peninsula, a forgotten chapter of industrial history
unfolds. The remnants of the Fiborn Quarry stand as a
testament to the region's once-thriving limestone industry.

95

In the early 20th century, the discovery of high-quality limestone in the area sparked the interest of entrepreneur Chase Osborn and railroad magnate William Foresman Fitch. Together, they formed the Fiborn Limestone Company and constructed a bustling quarry town. The town, complete with homes, a school, and a railroad spur, catered to the needs of the quarry's workforce.

The quarry operated for several decades, supplying limestone to various industries. However, the Great Depression brought an end to the company's prosperity. As demand for limestone dwindled, the quarry ceased operations in 1936, leaving behind a desolate landscape of concrete structures and scarred terrain.

Today, the ruins of the Fiborn Quarry are part of the Karst Preserve, a unique ecological area. Visitors can explore the abandoned buildings, marvel at the scale of the operation, and gain insight into the region's industrial past. A short hike leads to the site, offering a glimpse into a bygone era. While the quarry town is long gone, its ruins serve as a reminder of the human endeavor and the impact of industry on the natural world.

# Pequaming

Location:
Ford Dr.
L'Anse, MI 49946
46.8520553, -88.39838885

North of L'Anse, where the Keweenaw Bay curves into a sheltered embrace, lies a point of land rich in history. Once, the Ojibwe people called it Pequaming, meaning "headlands," and made their home there. In the late 19th century, Charles Hebard, a shrewd businessman, recognized the area's potential and established a bustling sawmill, employing hundreds and transforming the quiet point into a thriving lumber town.

The Hebard family's success caught the eye of another industrial titan Henry Ford. In 1922, Ford purchased the entire operation, captivated by the region's vast timber resources. Pequaming became a model company town, a testament to Ford's belief in self-reliance and education. New schools were built for the workers' children, and the grand bungalow, once a summer retreat for the Hebards, was repurposed as a winter vocational training center.

As the automobile industry evolved and shipping costs rose, the demand for lumber dwindled. In 1942, Ford closed the mill, and Pequaming's golden era came to an end. Today, the town is a quiet reminder of its industrial past. The brick powerhouse and the water tower, still adorned with the Ford logo, stand as silent sentinels. The historic bungalow, a symbol of both the Hebard and Ford legacies, continues to grace the shoreline, a testament to a bygone era. On a two track next to the cemetery stands the old Odd Fellows Hall. The buildings are still privately owned and not accessible to visitors but it is fun to drive around the town and wonder what it must have been like when Ford owned most of it.

The town is privately owned. Visitors can drive on the public streets but please do not enter any buildings. The nearby town of Alberta was an old Ford sawmill site that is maintained by Michigan Tech University.

# Ghost Town of Cliff

Location:
US-41 about five miles north of
the town of Mohawk
47.372814235, -88.31373292

Deep in the heart of the Keweenaw Peninsula, nestled
amidst towering pines and ancient rock formations, lies
the legendary Cliff Mine. A pioneering mine in the
Michigan Copper District, this historic site dates back to
1845, marking the beginning of a copper boom that

would shape the region's destiny. Legend has it that the mine was discovered by a hapless prospector who, after a tumble down a greenstone bluff, landed painfully on a protruding chunk of copper.

For over a decade, Cliff Mine reigned supreme as the largest copper producer in the United States. Its rich veins of copper fueled industrial progress and economic growth. However, as the ore deposits dwindled in the 1870s, the mine's operations ceased, leaving behind a ghost town etched into the landscape.

Today, visitors can still explore the stone ruins that once formed the backbone of this bustling community. The towering stone walls and foundations of buildings, now reclaimed by nature, stand as silent sentinels of the past. A particularly striking sight is a massive stone tower, likely a chimney, that rises above the forest floor.

To reach the Cliff Mine ruins, venture along the west branch of the Eagle River, following Cliff Drive. Look for a wooden sign marking the old mine, located in a parking area next to the road. A small, makeshift wooden bridge crosses the Eagle River near the mine's tailings piles. It's beyond these tailings that you'll find the historic chimney and stone walls.

# Vermillion Point

Location:
Lake Superior shoreline at the
end of N. Vermillion Road,
Paradise, MI 49768
46.7630771, -85.15198000

Before the modern U.S. Coast Guard, the U.S. Lifesaving Service was the first line of defense for sailors in distress on the Great Lakes. Among the most remote and challenging of these stations was Vermilion Point, a desolate outpost on the shores of Lake Superior. Dubbed

102

the "Alcatraz of the Lifesaving Service," the station was a harsh and isolated assignment for its crew.

Established in 1876, Vermilion Point was a lifeline for those lost or stranded on the treacherous waters. Supplies were delivered by boat during the warmer months and by dog sled in the harsh winter. The station's isolation made it a unique and challenging place to live and work. It remained operational until 1944, when it was abandoned and left to the mercy of the elements.

In the decades that followed, the property changed hands several times. Eventually, it was acquired by the Little Traverse Conservancy, which partnered with the nonprofit group S.O.S. Vermilion to preserve and restore the historic buildings. Today, visitors can explore the grounds of the former life saving station, marveling at the rugged beauty of the Lake Superior shoreline and imagining the lives of those who once called this remote outpost home. The buildings are not open to the public, but you can look through the windows to get a feel for life at this remote Upper Peninsula location.

While the journey to Vermilion Point is not for the faint of heart, the rewards are great. The winding, sandy road leading to the station offers a glimpse into the region's natural beauty. However, visitors should be aware that the road can be impassable during wet conditions, particularly in the spring. It's best to plan your visit during the summer or fall months when the weather is more stable.

Nearby is the Crisp Point Lighthouse. To reach the lighthouse go back to M-123 and follow the signs along Northwestern Road. Do not attempt to travel down the roads and trails along the shoreline because they become impassable for vehicles and ORVs.

# Peninsula Point Lighthouse

Location:
3722 County 513 T. Road
Rapid River, MI 49878
45.6682810, -86.96709533

The Stonington Peninsula, a rugged finger of land jutting into Lake Michigan, is a hidden gem in Michigan's Upper Peninsula. This remote location was once home to a vital beacon, the Peninsula Point Lighthouse.

105

Constructed in 1865, the modest yellow brick lighthouse served as a crucial navigational aid for ships traversing the Great Lakes. Reaching the lighthouse by land was a challenging endeavor, requiring a treacherous journey along a narrow footpath. Supplies were delivered by boat, making the lighthouse keeper's existence a solitary and often perilous one.

As maritime technology advanced, the lighthouse's role diminished. The construction of the Minneapolis Shoal Lighthouse in 1936 further reduced the need for Peninsula Point, leading to its decommissioning. The property was transferred to the National Forest Service, which made efforts to improve access and create a recreational area.

Despite these efforts, the lighthouse began to deteriorate. The keeper's house was lost to a fire in 1959, but the tower itself survived, thanks to the dedication of the Stonington Grange organization. Today, the lighthouse stands as a testament to the past, offering visitors a glimpse into a bygone era.

To reach this historic landmark, visitors must venture along a winding, two-track road through the dense forest. The journey, while challenging, is rewarded with stunning views of Lake Michigan from the top of the lighthouse tower. The tower is open for visitors to climb the winding staircase. The lamp is gone but the view from the top remains as awe inspiring today as it was when it was first constructed.

In the late spring the point is a stopping place for migrating monarch butterflies. The lighthouse is a popular place to visit at the end of September to see the traveling butterflies.

# Power House Falls

Location:
End of Power House Road
L'Anse, MI 49946
46.73712405, -88.44431707

Just south of L'Anse, nestled amidst the scenic beauty of Michigan's Upper Peninsula, lies Powerhouse Falls. This captivating waterfall, cascading down the Falls River, is a sight to behold. What sets it apart is its intriguing juxtaposition with an abandoned hydroelectric power plant, a relic of the region's industrial past.

The falls are easily accessible, with a well-maintained parking area and a short walk to the viewing area. The picnic tables scattered around the site offer a perfect spot to relax and soak in the serene atmosphere. The combination of the powerful waterfall and the historic power plant creates a unique and visually striking scene.

The old powerhouse adds a touch of industrial history to the natural beauty of the falls. Its weathered facade and rusting machinery contrast sharply with the pristine wilderness that surrounds it. This blend of nature and human ingenuity makes Powerhouse Falls a truly special place to visit.

# Nonesuch Mine

Location:
Porcupine Mountains Wilderness
State Park
Parking area off
South Boundary Rd.
46.7582592, -89.619629

The Porcupine Mountains, a vast wilderness in Michigan's Upper Peninsula, is a hiker's paradise, renowned for its rugged trails, cascading waterfalls, and the breathtaking Lake of the Clouds. Yet, hidden within its dense forests lies a forgotten chapter of the region's history: the ghost town of Nonesuch.

In the late 19th century, Nonesuch sprang to life as a mining town, fueled by the promise of copper riches. The town's unique name was derived from the type of copper ore found in the sandstone formations. At its peak, Nonesuch boasted a population of 300, with a school, boarding houses, stables, and even a baseball team.

However, the labor-intensive process of extracting copper from sandstone proved unsustainable. By 1912, the mine had closed, and the town gradually faded into obscurity.

Today, remnants of Nonesuch remain, scattered across the forest floor. Stone walls, rusted machinery parts, and other artifacts offer a glimpse into the past. Most intriguing is its stone mine shaft entrance.

To explore the ruins of Nonesuch, visitors can follow a short trail from a designated parking area. The trail winds through the woods, leading to the former mining site. As you wander through the overgrown landscape, you can imagine the bustling activity that once filled this quiet corner of the Porcupine Mountains.

# Bay Furnace

Location:
Bay Furnace Campground
E7900 W, M-28
Munising, MI 49862
46.4420239, -86.7055784

Located along the shores of Lake Superior, Bay Furnace Campground offers more than just a place to pitch a tent. It's a portal to the past, where the remnants of a bygone era stand as a testament to the region's industrial heritage.

113

Before it became a campground, the area was home to an Ojibwe fishing village known as Onota, meaning "the place where fishermen live." In the mid-19th century, the Bay Furnace Company transformed the landscape, constructing a massive iron smelting furnace. Grand Island provided a natural harbor, and the surrounding forests supplied ample firewood. The town that grew around the furnace was a bustling hub of activity, attracting workers from far and wide.

Tragedy struck in 1877 when a devastating fire swept through the town, destroying most of the buildings. The Bay Furnace Company never recovered, and the town gradually faded into obscurity. The area later became known as Christmas, a name derived from a short-lived toy factory.

Today, the ruins of the iron furnace stand as a poignant reminder of the past. The massive stone structure, weathered by time and the elements, offers a glimpse into the industrial might of a bygone era. Visitors can explore the site, marveling at the engineering feats of the past.

Whether you're a history buff or simply enjoy the beauty of the Great Lakes, a visit to Bay Furnace Campground is a must. As you wander through the ruins, you'll be transported back in time, to a period of industrial growth and decline.

# The Big Steam Engine

Location:
Trout Creek Twp. Park
102 Pine St,
Trout Creek, MI 49967
46.47726106, -89.01375732

Located on the west side of Michigan's Upper Peninsula, the quaint town of Trout Creek offers a unique glimpse into the region's industrial past. One of the town's most fascinating attractions is a massive steam engine, a relic of the era when steam power was the driving force behind manufacturing.

Located in Abbott Fox Community Park, the steam engine is a behemoth of machinery. Built in 1912 by Allis-Chalmers, this mechanical marvel once powered a flour mill in Minneapolis, Minnesota. In 1921, it was transported to Trout Creek and put to work in a local sawmill. For decades, the engine chugged away, powering the saws and other machinery that transformed raw timber into lumber.

While the sawmill is long gone, the steam engine remains. Its massive flywheel, measuring sixteen feet in diameter, is a testament to its power and size. It's a reminder of the industrial age, when steam-powered factories and mills shaped the landscape of the Upper Peninsula.

If you're traveling along M-28, be sure to take a detour to Trout Creek and marvel at this impressive piece of history. It's a captivating reminder of the ingenuity and hard work that built the region.

A few miles to the west on M-28 is Agate Falls Scenic Site. It is an impressive waterfall with a massive steel trestle train bridge that passes over it.

# Jackson Mine

Location:
Jackson Mine Park
199 Tobin St
Negaunee, MI 49866
Mine opening near
46.49832837, -87.6228258

Southwest of downtown Negaunee, a forgotten neighborhood known as Old Town lingers. Once a bustling community, it now exists as a haunting reminder of the past. The area is marked by a series of mysterious staircases that lead to nowhere, remnants of houses and buildings that once stood tall.

The rise of Old Town was tied to the discovery of iron ore in the region. In the mid-19th century, surveyor William Burt noticed unusual compass readings, leading to the discovery of rich iron ore deposits. The Jackson Mine, the first of its kind in the Lake Superior region, soon began operations.

As the mining industry flourished, Old Town grew. However, the decline of mining in the mid-20th century led to the gradual abandonment of the neighborhood. The unstable ground, riddled with old mine shafts, made the area unsafe for habitation. Buildings were demolished or relocated, leaving behind a ghostly landscape of crumbling foundations and overgrown lots.

Today, the area is part of a public park, and the Iron Ore Heritage Trail passes through its heart. Visitors can still explore the remnants of Old Town, wandering down the old streets and marveling at the forgotten staircases. A short trail leads to a fenced-off mine entrance, offering a glimpse into the subterranean world that once fueled the region's prosperity and it also includes old mining equipment on display near the parking area.

# Quincy Smelting Works

Location:
48991 Maple St,
Hancock, MI 49930
47.12658769, -88.56530061

Perched on the shores of Portage Lake, the Quincy Smelter stands as a testament to the region's rich mining history. This complex of industrial buildings, located north of Hancock in the Keweenaw Peninsula, once played a vital role in the production of copper.

The Quincy Mining Company constructed the smelter to process copper ore into pure copper ingots. These ingots were then shipped to factories around the world, where they were transformed into a variety of products, from copper wire to tubing. The smelter's strategic location on the shores of Lake Superior facilitated the transportation of both raw materials and finished products.

Today, the Quincy Smelter is the sole surviving copper smelter in the Lake Superior region and is part of the Keweenaw National Historical Park. A local nonprofit group, the Quincy Smelter Association, gives tours to the public in the summer months. You can find more info at https://quincymine.com/smelter-tour/

# Osborn Estate

Location:
Chase Osborn Preserve
on Sugar Island
46.358214435, -84.135677643

On the secluded Duck Island, a piece of Michigan history unfolds. Chase S. Osborn, a fascinating figure, left his mark on this idyllic island. He constructed two log cabins, aptly named Big Duck and Little Duck, along with a concrete library housing his extensive book collection.

Osborn's legacy extends beyond his island retreat. He served as the 27th Governor of Michigan and was the only governor to hail from the Upper Peninsula. Notably, he proposed the construction of a bridge across the Straits of Mackinac to President Roosevelt in 1939.

A curious log structure near the riverbank adds to the island's intrigue. While its exact purpose remains uncertain, it's speculated that it served as a private retreat or perhaps a shed. Osborn, known for his unconventional lifestyle, was said to have slept outdoors on a bed of pine boughs.

In 1927, Osborn donated his property to the University of Michigan, ensuring its preservation for future generations. His vast library was gifted to both the University of Michigan and Lake Superior State University.

A poignant reminder of Osborn's life can be found in the form of a large rock serving as a grave marker for him and his second wife, Stellanova. Their unconventional relationship, marked by a significant age difference, has added layers of mystery to their story.

Today, the property is known as the Chase S. Osborn Preserve, dedicated to research and education in natural sciences and forestry. While the main gate on S. Homestead Road is open to the public, visitors are reminded to respect the serene environment and adhere to the park's guidelines. A short hike leads to the historic estate, offering a glimpse into the life of this remarkable figure and his enduring legacy.

A ferry service, priced at $20 per vehicle, traverses the St. Mary's River to Sugar Island. The ferry dock is situated adjacent to Clyde's Drive Inn.

# Mansfield

Location:
Stream Road
Mansfield Township, MI 49920
46.11857802, -88.22013335

Nestled in the heart of Michigan's Upper Peninsula, the small town of Mansfield carries a poignant history marked by tragedy and resilience. A devastating mine collapse in 1893 claimed the lives of 27 miners, leaving a lasting scar on the community.

126

Today, only a few remnants of Mansfield remain. A charming log cabin church, lovingly restored by local historians, stands as a testament to the town's enduring spirit. This historic church, built in the late 1800s, served as a place of worship for the town's residents and continues to be used for special occasions.

Behind the church, the ruins of old cabins offer a glimpse into the past. These weathered structures, overgrown with vegetation, tell a story of a community that was once

vibrant and full of life. The mine disaster forced residents to flee their homes, leaving behind a ghost town that has been slowly reclaimed by nature.

A few miles northeast of Crystal Falls, a stone memorial commemorates the 27 miners who perished in the tragic mine collapse. This somber reminder serves as a tribute to the lives lost and the sacrifices made by these brave workers.

The town of Mansfield, though small and often overlooked, offers a unique opportunity to connect with the past. Its history, marked by both triumph and tragedy, continues to shape the identity of the Upper Peninsula.

# Clark Mine

Location:
Clark Mine Road
Mohawk, MI 49950
47.4452807, -87.86066352

Rising from the dense forest east of Copper Harbor, a solitary smokestack stands as a silent sentinel of the past. This imposing structure is all that remains of the Clark Mine, a once-thriving operation that played a significant role in the Copper Country's mining boom.

Established in 1853, the Clark Mine produced copper ore for decades. However, as the region's mining industry matured, the mine's profitability dwindled. By 1901, the Clark Mine had ceased operations, leaving behind a legacy of industrial activity and a stark reminder of the area's rich mining history.

Today, the abandoned mine site is a popular destination for rock hounds and history enthusiasts. The area is littered with rocks and stones, offering a glimpse into the geological processes that shaped the Copper Country. The smokestack, a towering relic of the past, provides a dramatic backdrop for exploring the site.

To reach the Clark Mine, visitors can follow Manganese Road east from the Copper Harbor Visitor Center. The road eventually turns into Clark Mine Road, A wooden sign points travelers to the site.

# Gay Mill

Location:
Gay Lac La Belle Road
Gay, MI 49945
47.2264676, -88.16180446

The town of Gay is located along the east side of the Keweenaw Peninsula. Its most well-known landmark is the Gay Bar, but a little ways down the road is a tall chimney. It was part of the old Mohawk and Wolverine Stamp Mill. Rail cars full of ore would come into the mill and dump the ore where it would be pulverized and the copper extracted. The remaining sand would be conveyed out to the Lake Superior shoreline. The mill operated from 1900 to 1932 and produced 22 million metric tons of sand. Over the decades the sand has eroded into Lake Superior affecting the spawning of trout and salmon. The state and EPA are working on relocating the sand and controlling the erosion.

When I was there taking photos a lady was placing a sign for the museum and invited me to come and see it. Near the chimney is an old two-story building that served as a school for many years. It has now been turned into a museum and there I learned a lot about the old stamp mill and the town of Gay. It was the first time I have ever been along the east side of the Keweenaw. I mostly travel up the west side to see Eagle Habor and Brockway Mountain. If you are ever in the Keweenaw be sure to take a trip along the east side. The road that travels along the lake is a beautiful drive and you can stop in the town of Gay and learn some history or get a drink at the Gay Bar.

Situated along the eastern shore of the Keweenaw Peninsula, the small town of Gay offers a glimpse into the region's rich mining history. While the Gay Bar may be its most famous landmark, the town's industrial past is equally fascinating.

A towering smokestack stands as a relic of the Mohawk and Wolverine Stamp Mill, a once-bustling facility that processed millions of tons of copper ore. Rail cars carrying ore would unload their cargo at the mill, where it was crushed and processed to extract valuable copper. The waste material, primarily sand, was then conveyed to the shores of Lake Superior.

Unfortunately, the erosion of this sand has had a negative impact on the local ecosystem, affecting the spawning grounds of trout and salmon. To mitigate this environmental issue, state and federal agencies are working to relocate the sand and control the erosion.

If you're planning a trip to the Keweenaw Peninsula, be sure to explore the eastern shore. The scenic drive along the coast offers stunning views of Lake Superior and the opportunity to discover hidden gems like the town of Gay. Whether you're interested in history, nature, or simply a good drink, the Keweenaw Peninsula has something for everyone.

# Freda Mill

Location:
Superior View Rd,
Atlantic Mine, MI 49905
47.13555515, -88.82116172

Along the rugged shoreline of Lake Superior, near the town of Freda in the Keweenaw Peninsula, stands a haunting reminder of the region's industrial past. A towering smokestack and a labyrinth of weathered concrete and twisted metal mark the site of the former Champion Mill.

This once-mighty mill played a crucial role in the Copper Country's mining boom. Trains laden with copper-rich rock would rumble into the mill, where the ore was pulverized and mixed with water from Lake Superior to create a copper-laden slurry. This slurry was then transported by rail to Houghton for further processing and ultimately transformed into copper ingots.

However, as the demand for copper declined, the Champion Mill ceased operations in 1967. The site was stripped of its valuable metals, leaving behind a skeletal framework of concrete and steel. Today, the ruins stand as a testament to the scale and power of the region's industrial heritage. Visitors can still appreciate its grandeur from a scenic overlook in Freda at the end of Superior View Road. It has a veterans memorial that provides stunning views of the ruins and the surrounding landscape.

Nearby, is the town of Redridge. A historic steel and wooden dam can be seen on the Salmon Trout River. The steel dam is one of three in the United States.

# Ahmeek Stamping Mill

Location:
51905 Spruce St,
Hubbell, MI 49934
47.16882809, -88.43535322

Along the winding roads of the Keweenaw Peninsula, a curious sight catches the eye: massive concrete blocks, towering over the landscape like ancient ruins. These remnants of the past are all that remains of the Ahmeek

Stamping Mill, a once-thriving industrial complex that played a crucial role in the region's copper mining boom.

Built in the early 1900s, the Ahmeek Stamp Mill was a marvel of engineering. Its towering concrete structures housed powerful stamping machines that pulverized copper ore into a fine sand. This process was essential to extracting the valuable copper from the rock.

Today, the mill ruins stand as a silent testament to the region's industrial heritage. The massive concrete blocks, weathered by time and the elements, offer a glimpse into the scale and complexity of the operation. The remaining fragments of the stamping machines, still visible atop the concrete foundations, hint at the powerful forces that once drove this industrial behemoth.

As you explore the site, you can't help but be awed by the sheer size of the structure. It's a reminder of the ingenuity and determination of the people who built and operated these mills, transforming the rugged landscape of the Keweenaw Peninsula into a center of industrial activity.

# Fort Wilkins

Location:
15223 US-41
Copper Harbor, MI 49918
47.4671891, -87.86168088

Perched at the northernmost tip of Michigan's Keweenaw Peninsula, the town of Copper Harbor offers a glimpse into a bygone era. Two centuries ago, this remote outpost was at the heart of a copper mining boom. To protect this valuable resource and maintain peace with local Native

American tribes, the U.S. government established Fort Wilkins in 1844.

Named after Secretary of War, William Wilkins, the fort boasted 27 structures, including a guardhouse, powder magazine, officers' quarters, barracks, mess halls, a hospital, a bakery, and a blacksmith's shop. However, the fort's existence was short-lived. After just two years, it was deemed unnecessary and abandoned, with the exception of Sergeant William Wright, who remained as a solitary caretaker until his death in 1855.

The fort saw a brief resurgence after the Civil War, serving as a place for soldiers to complete their enlistments. It's easy to imagine the discontent of soldiers stationed in such a remote and harsh environment, especially during the frigid winter months. By 1870, the fort was once again abandoned.

In 1923, Fort Wilkins and the nearby lighthouse were designated as a state park. Thanks to the efforts of the Works Progress Administration (WPA) in the 1930s, the remaining original buildings were restored, and many others were reconstructed. A campground and shower facilities were also added, transforming the site into a popular destination for outdoor enthusiasts.

Today, Fort Wilkins Historic State Park offers visitors a unique opportunity to step back in time and experience the life of a frontier soldier. The well-preserved buildings and serene natural surroundings create a captivating atmosphere, inviting exploration and reflection.

The flag that flies over the historic fort is a twenty-six star flag. The design would have been the nation's flag in 1844 when the fort was constructed.

# Old Victoria

Location:
25401 Victoria Dam Rd,
Rockland, MI 49960
46.7034001, -89.22824951

Southwest of Rockland, Michigan, lies the historic townsite of Old Victoria. Founded in 1899 as a bustling mining town for the Victoria Copper Mining Company, it once hummed with activity. However, as the copper boom waned, so too did the town's fortunes. By 1921, Victoria was abandoned, its buildings left to decay and be reclaimed by nature.

The town's forgotten past began to resurface in 1965 when a dedicated group of local residents embarked on a mission to restore the historic site. Through their tireless efforts, the once-abandoned town was revived, transforming into a captivating museum that offers a unique glimpse into the region's rich mining heritage.

As visitors step into Old Victoria, they are transported back in time. Some of the buildings, and houses have been restored and stand as testament to the lives of those who once called this place home. Other structures remain in a dilapidated and abandoned state for visitors to marvel at and wonder about the challenges of living in a remote part of the Upper Peninsula.

# Fayette

Location:
4785 II Rd,
Garden, MI 49835
45.7180130, -86.66897674

Nestled on the Garden Peninsula, a serene finger of land jutting into Lake Michigan, lies the historic town of Fayette. This once-thriving iron smelting community, now a part of Fayette Historic State Park, offers a captivating glimpse into the past.

143

Founded in 1867 by the Jackson Iron Company, Fayette was strategically located in Snail Shell Harbor, providing an ideal setting for iron production and shipping. The town was named after one of the company's directors, Fayette Brown. In its heyday during the late 1800s, Fayette boasted a population of over 500 residents, most of whom were employed by the iron company.

At the heart of the town's industry was the iron furnace, where iron ore was smelted to produce pig iron. This

intermediary product, more efficient to transport than raw ore, was crucial to the steel industry. The name "pig iron" is a curious one, stemming from the ingots' resemblance to piglets.

However, the decline of the timber industry and the emergence of more efficient iron and steel production methods led to the town's eventual demise. By the early 1890s, Fayette was forced to shut down, leaving behind a ghost town.

Today, Fayette State Park preserves the town's rich history. Nineteen original buildings, including homes, a general store, a schoolhouse, and the iconic iron furnace, have been stabilized. The doors of the buildings are open so visitors can wander through these historic structures, imagining the lives of the people who once called Fayette home.

# Conclusion

The adage "the only constant is change" rings true in the ever-evolving landscape of Michigan. As new structures rise, older ones are often abandoned, destined for demolition or preservation. It is a testament to our collective history when historic buildings are saved from the wrecking ball and repurposed for the future.

A prime example of such a transformation is Detroit's Michigan Central Station. Once the largest train depot in the United States, it fell into disrepair after passenger service ceased in the 1960s. Decades later, Ford Motor Company breathed new life into the iconic building, renovating it into a modern office space.

It is my hope that these abandoned sites, each with its unique story, will continue to stand as reminders of Michigan's rich history. By preserving these historic landmarks, we ensure that future generations can appreciate and learn from the past.

Continue following
my journey at

www.lostinmichigan.net


To follow my travels outside of
Michigan you can visit

www.lostinthestates.com

Other Books by Mike Sonnenberg

Lost In Michigan Volumes 1-7
Lost In Michigan's Upper Peninsula
Lost In Michigan's Ghost Towns
Lost In Ohio
Lost In Indiana
Lost In Illinois
Lost In Wisconsin
Light From The Birdcage